# HOME TRUTHS

by Ryan Guth

TRANSCENDENT ZERO PRESS
HOUSTON, TEXAS

PUBLISHED BY TRANSCENDENT ZERO PRESS
*www.transcendentzeropress.org*

ISBN-13: 978-1-946460-02-8

Library of Congress Control Number: 2018943062

Cover design by Glynn Monroe Irby
Cover photograph is the author's grandmother's house

Printed in the United States of America

Transcendent Zero Press
16429 El Camino Real Apt. 7
Houston, TX 77062

Authoritative Edition

# HOME TRUTHS

by Ryan Guth

# ACKNOWLEDGEMENTS

I suppose most writers would jump at the chance to make their early work more fit for public consumption, so I feel especially compelled to offer some pleases and thank-yous for the opportunity. I'm indebted first and last to Dustin Pickering of Transcendent Zero Press, for taking on this project and seeing it through so meticulously. Thanks are also due to Dr. Nell Senter for helping me negotiate the documentary minefield of copyright transfer; to Katie Howerton and the staff of *Our Jackson Home*, in which the revised edition of "Family Romance" made its first appearance in print; and to Mikayla Bazzell who performed, uncomplainingly, the mind-numbing task of preparing an electronic manuscript from the first edition, making it possible for me to do my tinkering with it. Equally necessary are the teachers in whose poetry workshops many of these pieces were born and nurtured: Andrew Hudgins, Don Bogen, and Christopher Buckley. I hope they will be pleased with the ways in which I have continued to learn from them in the years since I was in their classrooms. My assistant, Christine Hamilton, has used her extraordinary fluency in the new languages of social media and the internet to tirelessly promote my work in ways I've given up trying to understand, but am mighty grateful for. Lastly, acknowledgement is due to my circle of supportive first readers: Rebecca Yancey, Debra Tayloe, Richard Spring, Mark Walls, Robert Lavett Smith, Spencer Guth...

and, of course, Elizabeth.

*for Spencer,*
*just like last time*

# PREFACE

No worries if you want to skip this part (I don't usually read prefaces, either). But for anyone who might be interested, here's a bit of backstory on the present volume.

*Home Truths*, as it appears here, is both the same as and different from the first edition published in 2006 by Alsop Review Press. It tells the same story(ies), preserves the same memories and speculations, attempts the same themes. On the other hand, I have retouched every page – probably every stanza and/or paragraph. Most of the changes are too minute to mention, but I did convert a few pieces from one "genre" of text to another, and even altered the sequence of pieces, mostly in Parts III and IV.

The most significant difference, though, and the primary reason for this second edition, is the inclusion of five entirely new pieces. When a dear friend of our family, Mr. Dana W. Stockbridge, died a few years ago, I inherited packet of letters to him from my father, written during the time when he was working for my grandmother. These letters shed some additional light on that relationship, as well as his thoughts about the personal and professional circumstances in which he found himself. The four prose pieces "Responsibilities," "Squatters," "The Sooner the Better," and "Poison Ivy" are distilled from that correspondence.

The fifth "new" piece, "The Dead Shall Be Raised Incorruptible", is actually an old one. Apparently intended for the 2006 publication, it somehow got misfiled and was only rediscovered when I was looking for material for another project. It too has been substantially revised for this new – and now authoritative – edition of *Home Truths*.

*Radnor, Pennsylvania*
*Christmas Day, 2017*

# Contents

**IV.Truths**

## BLACK AND WHITE: THREE SNAPSHOTS
*Dayton, Ohio: 1954*

### 1.

A steep hill strewn with gravestones
walls off the back of the picture. Midground,
Hank – young man
in a houndstooth sportcoat –
squats by the pond's edge.
                              Behind him
Mildred, his mother-in-law, stands
holding a spray of flowers for her husband.

They might be sculpture, these two:
hand-worked surfaces the light rests on
but cannot penetrate.

### 2.

Back home, Phyllis and Hank
(still newly-weds, almost)
in the back yard. Un-
cooperative, he's
kept his shades on,
jammed his right hand
so deep in the pocket of his blazer
the sleeve's wrinkled
clear to the elbow.
What's he after –
notebook? car-keys? cigarettes?
He'd crush the pack,
from the look of him.
                              At his side,
a full head shorter, Phyllis
smiles and smiles for her mother
taking the picture. Mildred's shadow,
long as a giant's in the late afternoon,
almost reaches their feet....

All the time in the world.

3.

Mildred, alone,
posing beside the chrome
jawbone and tusks
of the Cadillac Meteor
combination ambulance and hearse
Bob paid cash for, brand-new,
the year before he died. A standard shift,
to save some money.
                    Yet now
there's nobody but Hank (or sometimes Tom)
to drive it. Nobody else could keep the thing
from bucking like a colt off a popped clutch
in front of a funeral procession.
One more thing to worry about....

Behind her,
the upper stories of her house
dissolve into the scuffed white gloss
of a fifty-year-old sky.

# I. Home

# FAMILY LORE

"Daddy says you never paid him
when he worked here,"
I informed my grandmother
just before lunch. I was seven,
sitting at her feet
with a new yellow Tonka truck
and a cold that had kept me
out of school.
                    "Oh,
she sighed, "I paid him...."

She'd agreed to watch me
while he waited for our car
at the repair shop down the street
                              but now
*Another World* was coming on. Her flabby,
powder-dusted arm stretched
rippling over my head
as she turned the volume up
on her kitchen TV.
Organ chords throbbed.
                         Ab-
sently, she
scratched a flake of scaly
skin off her ankle.
I was losing her.
                  "Well..."
I tried, in my deepest voice –
"well, how much?"

        ৯

I knew already, though,
how she'd grown fat off his hard work: sitting
upstairs in the air-conditioning,
while all the chores she'd given him
(driving the hearse, mowing the lawn,
toting flowers and folding chairs
and vacuuming the chapel

after every funeral) had left him
too little time
to work on his writing.
                    Just at the point,
he said, when his agent needed to see
that he could keep producing steadily.


        ✍


My throat hurt.
I hated bread with oleo. And I'd just
pulled a wheel off my truck.
                    "How much?"
I asked again.
            This time
the dragon squirmed,
uncoiled a little.
Sighing through her nose,
she stared down at me for a moment,
searching my face –
I could see light from the window behind her
through her thinning hair –
then turned back to her program.

"That's between your father and me."

# MAKESHIFT I: *Flight*

Here's a sawed-off
hunk of broom handle
glazed with Stanley's Glue:
hand-grip and spindle.
Black-enameled
coat-hanger wire
bent into a bail.
Pegboard side-plates.
A tinkertoy rod
spinning on its
wood-screw axle
for a crank-handle.
                    No
satirical, post-
modern assemblage, this,
but a working kite reel
my father made for me
when I was five.
I remember it
rattling, sure and steady
in my small hands, till
all at once the line –
a quarter-mile
of thin white cotton
package string – snapped off
a foot from the spool,
wrapped itself around
a power line and dragged
our red and yellow box-kite
cartwheeling down
in spectacular, majestic
destruction: paper
skin burst, ribs
shattered, a small rain
of shreds and splinters
falling from the sky....

The string alone took us an hour
to untangle and rewind.

## THE PRESENCE OF THE PAST

Clear at the back of my grandmother's attic – that barn of a space on the third floor, cluttered with mildewed chairs, half-empty trunks, old garment bags like enormous cocoons hung from the ceiling – there was one more door, not much taller than I was at seven or eight, that opened onto... well, hardly a room. Not even a closet. A leftover, really: just about the size and shape of a pup-tent, with its own tiny window in the far wall. Spanning the open joist-work was a narrow bridge of water-stained, unsanded flooring planks. More planks, a whole stack of them, sat warped and swelling under the eaves, still waiting to be nailed down – as if the builder, instead of finishing his work, had simply let it trail off into empty space....

Bored, sometimes, with the endless recirculation of family stories around the holiday dinner table, I could go up there and gather wool for hours. In winter, frost formed on the rafters. In summer the musty, shut-in heat hit your face like an open hand. But you could lie down on that strip of floor, in a litter of crisp dead flies and hornets, and ride whatever weather was blowing through. September thunderstorms were the best – loose, leathery shingles flapping on both sides of you, the agonized howl of wind shattering itself against the eaves as the small square pane above your head filled up with whirling cloud-flak: blue, then purple, then almost black. Sometimes, too, the whole great frame of the house would seem to shudder briefly beneath you as it gathered strength enough to continue its own slow parallactic drift, out of talk and recollection, onward

and onward

and onward

into the present.

## MAKESHIFT II: *Perpetual Maintenance*

Snowmelt and leaky foundations
kept my father busy
every spring: sweeping
lakes of iron-cold water
over the basement floor
with a brush broom,
spooning loosened mortar sand
back into the weeping
cracks it had washed through.

I could hear him down there,
raging against the malicious
purposes of weather,
cinder-block walls,
landlords. In our old house
he was everywhere, in every room,
rumbling
like the voice of God
up through the furnace ducts.

When he yelled for me to bring him a dustpan,
the screws in the floor-grates rattled.

## THE LADY FUNERAL DIRECTOR AT WORK

"First job we've had in two-three weeks and it's
  an autopsy! I was so disgusted. You know,
  it used to be they'd leave the body alone
  'less there was some good reason. But not no more!
  These doctors now, they got to do their cutting
  no matter what – even if they have
  the cause of death already! It's too darn bad
  nobody ever tells US what they're doing.
  Sure as you're born, I'm going to have to pay
  the embalmers extra to put him back together,
  and they don't care if I gave prices
  to the family already. I'll be lucky
  if we break even!
                    Oh honey, it's not your fault.
  Your Grandma's just upset."

## MAKESHIFT III: *Perpetual Motion*

At forty-nine, my father
took up running:
measured out the length
of a lap around our basement
(58 to a mile),
bought himself a pair of
narrow-heeled track shoes and
disappeared for three hours
every weekday morning,
filling his lungs with sawdust
and the sweet black
reek of potato-rot –
ignoring the doorbell,
the telephone, the novel
he'd stayed home ten years
to write.
        Off-limits,
he said. Thinking,
he said, of the steady,
day-long lope
of a mountain wolf...
that soft *scuff-scuff*
of nubbled rubber
soles on concrete
broken only when

at the end of each half mile

he doubled back,
reversing his orbit.

## HURRICANE WILMA

I used to love it when
she'd push her upper denture plate
out with her tongue to scare me:
a grin broken free of the flesh,
all moist shiny teeth and pink gums....

      ❧


"One day I said to myself,
  'I'll never be rich, I'll never be famous,
  and God knows I was never any good
  at picking men!' So I decided
  if I wanted seconds on the stuffing
  or another piece of pie, then
  I was going to have it!"
                      "So of course
she wouldn't fit in the MRI machine.
They couldn't tell where-all
the cancer might have spread."

      ❧


"In high school, once she got in
  with those servicemen from Wright Field,
  seemed like she was out, oh,
  put-near every night. I remember
  Mother and Daddy sitting up
  till one or two in the morning,
  waiting for her to come in."

      ❧


"She married too young,
  that's all. She was taking care of us
  while all her friends were still out having fun.
  That's why she's wild now: just
  making up for what she missed."

      ❧

Wilma (a name she hated)
Graham
      Brewer
Swinford
      Rowinski
Johnson


&#8766;


Looking over her glasses at me,
her whiskey-deepened contralto theatrically
quiet,
conspiratorial:
      "You know, Ryan,
you're the only person in the world
that can call me Aunt."


&#8766;


"One time when we was girls, she got in my doll box. Mother and Daddy give us each a box of real nice dolls for Christmas one year, and I always tried to keep mine nice and neat, you know....But here I open up my box and there was grass-stains on half of them's clothes! And mud, and some kind of – I don't know, looked like dried-on ketchup or something in their hair. Anyway, it was all red and sticky. Well sir, I was so darn mad I couldn't see straight! So I went and got HER box. 'Cause she had this one doll she really liked: had a big china head, and hair like hers. Real long, you know, and kind of reddish-brown. Anyway, I just grabbed it and run up to the third floor. Don't know what I thought I's going to do – she'd about made me crazy, I guess. And she come a-running up the stairs behind me: 'Don't you touch my doll! Don't you dare!' So I turned right around and THREW the darn thing at her. That big head hit the step right in front of her face and smashed to smithereens... oh, it was perfect! She just stood there, stock still. Staring at me like she couldn't believe I had the nerve. Tell you the truth, I couldn't believe it either!"


&#8766;

"Phyllis always comes so well-
   prepared, but Wilma never has
   her music learned. And yet she is
   so good she gets away with it.
   I almost hate to put her in
   the recital. She and Phyllis are
   my two best pupils, but knowing
   that won't do her any good as
   far as applying herself."

                 ⁂

Listening to Bette and Amanda
belting out "The Rose" – their voices
blended like flame and heat – Aunt Wilma
turned to my mother and said
                              "That song just
PULLS the harmony out of you,
doesn't it?"
                 Then, to demonstrate,
put down her cigarette and
sang another inner voice
up into the arrangement:

improvised,
perfect.

                 ⁂

Weeping drunk,
   she called to break the news
   to each of us in turn –
   Dad, Mom, then me –
   that Elvis was dead.

                 ⁂

   …story of her
   phoning their father
   in the middle of the night:
   "Tom's going to hit me, Daddy,

22

please come help!"
                        I want him
to have taken the hearse, of course:
double-clutching through stop signs, cherry-top
strobing erratically on sidewalks, mailboxes,
parked cars. I can picture him
stumbling up their porch steps, hearing a slap –

then laughter from the open
bedroom window:
                        "Willie?"
he'd have called out.
                        "Oh shit!
Daddy? Is that you? It's okay,
we made up. I'd let you in, but"
– giggling –
"I'm not dressed!"


        ✍


... story of her
showing up at the funeral home
in the middle of a service: black eye,
bloodied nose....


        ✍


Dropping off the groceries she'd asked for
(the temp service hadn't called in three weeks),
Dad saw a man he didn't know
at her kitchen table, pouring himself
a glass of Mr. Boston. From the bedroom
another male voice, just audible
above the living-room TV –
turned up so loud the thin walls shook.
Her daughters,
huddled under a blanket on the sofa,
wouldn't look away from the screen.

Wouldn't say a word.


        ✍

And yet she straightened her ass right up
 after her only grandson was born:
 not a drop, not another
 husband or boyfriend or police encounter
 in the last twelve years of her life.

≈

The stone her children paid for,
 carved as she'd instructed:

*W. Elaine Graham*
*1932-1991*

## MAKESHIFT IV: *Soundproofing*

1.

I must have been in school
the day Dad carried my BB gun
up to his office, flung the window open
and potshot at our next-door neighbor's dog
for half an hour.
                              It had woken him up again.
And once he was awake,
   his nights were full of sound:
the growling of refrigerator trucks
in the Royal Crest Dairy's parking lot
across the street; a locomotive whistle
at the Trotwood crossing, two miles off;
a passenger-jet descending
to the airport in Vandalia. Worst of all,
the deep jug-flute of wind
across our chimney-stack
that meant a storm was coming.
He'd sit up till dawn
in our living room: no lights on,
only the television's
twitchy blue flickers and shadows
flittering like bats across the walls,
a bottle of Thunderbird or Gallo Sauterne
squatting by the pipe-rack on his end-table.

2.

He'd sawed off every tree branch
less than a foot from the house.
He'd tacked down the slack
in our power line. He'd asked the dairy
to move their trucks, then asked my mother
to ask them again. He'd called
and called and called
about that goddam dog.
                              So imagine
his satisfaction at seeing it, stung with BB's,
leaping and leaping against
its short, cruel chain.

## UNK

### 1.

*I always think of him in sunlight:*

*a drowsy old man,*
*whistling as he clears dead stems*
*and roots from the family urn,*
*pours in fresh black potting soil, then*
*breaks a dozen red-fringed coleus seedlings*
*out of their pasteboard cups and*
*pushes them, one by one,*
*down into the bed he's made for them….*

### 2.

Around us in the summer sun, three pink stones
shimmered. His father, his mother,
a baby sister –
                          "I still remember
seeing them pennies on her eyes.
That's what they used to do, you know,
take and put pennies on a corpse's eyes to close 'em.
Poor little thing. Only lived six weeks,
now ain't that awful?
You can go ahead and water now."

I held the hose at my crotch
and pretended to be a grown man peeing.
He didn't notice,
but broke a white chip off the side of the urn
and muttered something about new paint.
I saw the orange-red sores of rust
at the lip, where leaves had touched
or soil leached up: small splits and blisters
bleeding down the chalky sides.

My great-uncle Harold.
My grandmother's older brother,
"Unk" to all the family
since the day my oldest cousin, aged two, piped up
"Hi, Unc... Unc..."
and couldn't work her mouth

26

around the rest of it.

                What a name –
the kind of noise you'd make
if a car-door hit you in the stomach: *Unk*.

He always bought his shirts a size too large,
to leave room for the back brace
he'd been wearing faithfully
since long before I was born. Slipped disc.
Doctors at the hospital told him
he'd only need it for the first six months

but the pain, he said, had been so bad
he was frightened of it ever coming back.

"Just don't feel safe no more
without it on. Old Unk, he's funny...."

I suppose he was, at that. Wifeless, childless,
yet something of both himself, he seemed
content to drift along in the family's wake,
living with his mother until she died
then moving in with my grandmother,
widowed and running her husband's funeral home
at the corner of Wayne and Erie Avenues.
He had a job of his own –
three days a week, through the growing season –
as chief gardener on a rich man's family estate.
Then spent his winters with a sister-in-law in Florida
who paid his airfare there and back each Christmas.

        3.
Grandma always said
that Unk had been their mother's favorite.
Mostly, she believed, because
their father had thought so little of him:
*no damn good for catching*
*pigs or girls, that one.*
*And dumb as a post besides!*

27

4.

My parents bought their first and only house
when I was fourteen. I had a pet redbud –
the sole survivor
of half a dozen I'd picked up at school fundraisers
over the years. The only one
I hadn't starved to death by over-pruning,
poisoned with bug spray or left
to wilt, un-watered, in the summer heat.
It was five years old and taller than I was,
so I wanted to take it with us when we moved.
But every nursery I called
advised against it:
                    "You can't take up a tree
mid-August. It's in leaf – the shock'd kill it.
Them redbuds are delicate, you know."
Unk neither agreed nor disagreed with this advice,
and ventured no predictions of his own.
But since he'd mowed my grandmother's lawn that week
and visited the family graves in Piqua,
there wasn't much else needed doing,
so he said he'd give it a try.
                            Next morning,
he was out in the yard before I woke up:
digging a trench around my tree
and severing every root he found
with lopping shears. I helped him
rock the smooth trunk back and forth,
bending it further and further over
until its heart-shaped leaves touched the grass
and a few last root-strings snapped.
                            By noon,
we had it standing in its new spot.
                            "Lots of sunlight there,"
he observed.
                    "Is that all right?"
He shook his head.
                    "I don't expect it matters."
Then he explained what WAS important:
water.

"You want a stream
about as thick as your finger, no more.
Take and put your hose right down there in the dirt
and let it run for half an hour.
Maybe an hour, today."
If water pooled around the roots, he said,
they'd drink it up
and stay right where they were.
A good long soak, on the other hand,
went deep into the ground
and made the roots go after it.
And THAT was what you wanted.


     5.
I followed his instructions to the letter,
but in less than a week
the leaves all withered anyway, green on the branch,
and dropped away.
               One afternoon,
on his way home from the cemetery,
Unk was hit broadside by a drunk in a pick-up truck
and thrown against his car-door. Five ribs broken,
a month in the hospital. Released,
he was terrified of falling: especially in the bathtub,
with its jutting knobs and faucets
so much harder than his old bones.
Having trained himself to sponge-wash
at the sink instead, he forgot one night
and drew a bath, stepped in…
then couldn't make himself sit down.
                    "Ain't this a sight?"
he cried: his back to us,
hands pressed against the tiles.
               "I guess
my sister called you?"
             She had.
Dad told me to take Unk's arm. He shied away
at first, then slowly stretched one hand out,
giving me his weight. Dad knelt
and ran some good hot water onto his wash-cloth.

6.

That winter was mild – two or three light snows
that melted off in a few days,
even the plow-piles by the roads. Unk mended,
made his trip to Florida, and got back
just in time to see my tree
all broken out in leaf-buds.
Bending down a pimpled branch
to test its spring, he let it
whip back upright, stirring the others.
                              "Don't expect
you'll need to water it this year, do you?
I guess I'll go in now."


7.

*I watch him*
*watching his own slow footsteps*
*through the grass.*
*Hands held out at his sides*
*for balance, he seems to wade*
*through pools of evening light.*

*Harold Van Emon Daganhardt*
*1897-1982*

# STAND UP AND SING

A trained musician, my mother could open up a hymnal in our pew at the Fort McKinley United Methodist Church and sight-read the alto line from any selection, whether or not she'd ever performed it before. In those days, she was also working about fifty hours a week as a secretary in the medical office of Inland Manufacturing, so my father could stay home and write. Usually she got up and left the house before Dad or I were even awake, and didn't get home again till dark. Most of those nights, she'd fall asleep in front of the TV an hour or so after dinner.

Altos never have the tune, you understand. They're assigned an odd inner part, a sort of harmonic shadow for the melody above them. But let that melody go off-key – which it always does, in any congregation singing – and the alto will sound like the one who got it wrong. I was used to people glancing over at us: puzzled, startled, annoyed. One time, a little girl with shiny blue ribbons in her hair turned all the way around in front of me and whispered, "Why don't she sing the right song?"

I don't know why. She didn't seem to care about (or even notice) those reactions to her harmonizing. I guess she did it simply because she could: because she was good at it, she knew she was good at it, and it was the only opportunity she had at that point in her life to make use of her gifts.

However you can, stand up and sing.

*Phyllis Joanne Guth*
*1929-2004*

# II. Artifacts

## THE GHOST AT HOME
*a snapshot of my grandfather, Christmas 1952*

On my grandmother's kitchen table,
the holiday meal is almost ready.
A jello mold, some bowls of salad,
that big old earthenware
crock I remember,

full of buttered oyster dressing.
Over by the stove there's Bob,
caught in the act: lips greasy,
a shred of turkey still in his hand.
Not even smiling – is he about to,

or will he be annoyed? Whoever
took the picture would have known.
To me, it feels wrong
seeing him there,
in that familiar room. To me,

the only thing he's ever been
is his death just ten months later:
that enormous,
irresistible event-horizon
pulling time and memory and his family

in after him, forever. Some,
like my parents,
from hundreds of miles away,
from different lives, different work.
And now me, decades later,

to try and understand.

*Robert C. Graham*
*1897-1953*

# USEABLE FAMILY

27 March 1952

Dear Phyllis:

Herewith, my attempt to do the chores you assigned me in your last letter. You should know going into this thing, though, that my previous existence – previous to meeting you, I mean – isn't worth the typewriter ribbon I'm about to waste on it.

I think I told you already that my mother (first name: Christina, maiden name: Klein – I think) died when I was ten. That and the Great Depression put my father (also a Henry) permanently out of commission as a provider. Not that he ever showed much talent in that line. What I didn't tell you was that he installed my brother Fred and me in a local orphanage while he skedaddled off to Nevada with our mother's insurance money. He sunk the cash in a silver mine that went bust a year or so later, and never came back for us. So Fred and I ended up at a foster home in Orwell, Ohio: the Justice and Mrs. Arnett. The county paid them for our room and board, on top of which they made lavish use of us as free labor on their truck farm. Somebody forgot to tell them about the Emancipation Proclamation.

What's this family history for, anyway? A simple newspaper wedding announcement goes two lines at a buck or so a line. You aren't trying to run with the Morgan and Rockefeller crowd, I hope. Save the space. Tell 'em I was born, I pounded a telegraph key in Panama during WWII, and my principal occupations are writing and loving you.

Speaking of writing, I've got some pretty big news. You read this particular yarn (the one about the Martian microbes), so you might be interested to know that some lousy rag called *Esquire* actually laid out a little cold harsh cash for it. In fact, they're running it in the April issue!

As if that weren't enough, my agent also sold the rights for it to a television show called "Tales of Tomorrow." Rumor is it's going to be on next month. This TV angle is one I never considered, although I figured my agent might eventually push some stories into Hollywood. But that's all daydreaming, and I prefer to see things as they are. For now, I write for the magazines, even though it looks like I've officially graduated from pulps like *Planet Stories*.

And the writing itself is going like gangbusters. Four more pieces in the mill or being thrashed out with Dana, who I assume you'll remember. That confounded Simon Legree keeps inventing complications – good ones, I mean – for my characters. Pitiful pasts and hidden hardships. Then it's my job to decide how that'll make them act in a given situation. He's trying to make some kind of heart-wrecking Russian novelist out of me, but such enrichments are probably what moved me up to the likes of *Esquire*. For now, he's the other half of my writing brain, although eventually I need to be able to do his part on my own.

Back to work (one of my more useful rejection slips warned me about my tendency to digress. I once sent my sister a short note, but she mistook it for a bale of old phone directories and flung it in the furnace!)

I'm not sure how many names I can supply for that guest list other than my brother, my sisters, and my reprobate old man – who certainly won't have the scratch to make such a trip even if he did want to. I suppose the Arnetts will have to be invited. Between you, me, and the typewriter, though, I hope theirs gets lost in the mail. I'm going to send you the addresses of a couple of Dana's relatives, however. Most of them are probably too old to travel so far, and they only know me as a friend of their nephew or cousin or whatever he is to them. But they were good folks and kind to me, so I'd appreciate your wasting a stamp or two on them.

Don't feel badly, by the way, about my lack of useable family. I've got you, which (who?) is (are?) all the family I need. You're the one with the goldarned college edjimacaishkun; I'll let you figure out the grammar.

Only a few more eons of torture then you and I will be an us.

In agonies and torments of yearning,

(Hank)


*Black fine-point fountain pen, on plain 8.5 x 11" sheet folded in half width-wise. Hand slightly shaky but clear, the lines of text reasonably clear.*

## THE DEAD SHALL BE RAISED INCORRUPTIBLE

1. *November 10, 1952*

Dear Phyllis,

A few more wedding gifts came here that you will need to acknowledge

silver bonbon dish from Mrs. Harris
hideaway can opener from Louise Mitchell and children
2 Fire King baking dishes (Russells)
monopoly set (Aunt Amy – wouldn't you know!)

————

Also found this note when going through your Grandma's things today
and thought you would want to have it. I guess it wasn't finished, since
there isn't any signature. But it's dated 4 months before she died. I guess
she must have just lost track of it. It was sitting under a pile of mending
on her kitchen table. Hope you and Hank are keeping well.

Love
Mother

*Heavy penciled writing, on a cut-down sheet of ledger paper
(both sides printed with a grid pattern in brown, green and
light blue inks; 2 punched holes near bottom edge).*

*2. June 7, 1952*

Dear Phyllis

Our roses are in bloom and
they are so beautiful. Not near as
many as there were last year, for it
was so cold in January they froze
pretty bad even tho' your uncle
Harold fixed them up some with
Wood chips. Wish you were here I
would put one in your hair. We
have five different colors

*Black fine-point fountain pen, on plain 8.5 x 11" sheet*
*folded in half width-wise. Hand slightly shaky but clear,*
*the lines of text reasonably straight.*

# TOO BIG

Phyl:

Here's a little loot. If you need more, I'll try to scrape it up.

I'm pooped. Bushed. Fagged. Weary. Don't know if I can lick a stamp, let alone type out a letter. Going over to Dana's place tomorrow night, ostensibly for a story conference – but probably with empty hands and heart because anxiety over Dad has thrown my writing schedule completely out of kilter for the last several weeks. I've thought of practically nothing else but this tragedy since I got back from the funeral – it haunts me. Like being shattered by a bomb.

How is mother? Give her my love. I'm glad to hear Uncle Harold got a new Plymouth. If any man ever deserved a shiny new car, he's that man. He's remarkable.

So are you. Thanks for telephoning to keep me informed. I depend on you. I miss you. I love you so much I can't even understand it any more. Too big.

Return as soon as you possibly can.

(Love,

(Hank)

*Typed (except for closing and signature) on 8.5" x 11" typing paper: green, no watermark. Again, no errors are discernible.*

# THE CAST IS ASSEMBLED

1. *November 1, 1953*

Dear Phyllis,

It is now 25 minutes to one in the morn. I went to lodge meeting this eve. Got home at 12:05, drank a bottle of Stroh's and went down and put Mrs. Glotfelter's hair up in pin curls. I do hope she'll look natural. You remember she had cancer. She was very bad, couldn't get out of bed the last month or so. You wouldn't have recognized her when they brought her in. She had a prearrangement with Daddy so no money from it.

Had your Uncle Harold over to dinner last night. I think he's going to ask if he can move in here now that your grandmother's house is sold. That would be all right with me. He brought a steak for each of us, and I sat out the leftover baked beans from last nite. Only had green onions and icicle radishes for a relish tray. Coffee, rolls and butter and some Scherer's ice cream. I even ate the fat around my steak. Ha! Your daddy would have got a kick out of that. He stayed here till 9 pm. We watched the boxing on TV, then he went home.

I am thinking very seriously of trying to make an embalmer out of Tom. His gas station isn't doing any too well. He and your sister are back together, or did she tell you already? I'm not sure he could handle the school part, but you should see him when I ask him to help with a body. He really eats it up. I have to say he's been a big help these past few weeks.

Love
Me

PS: I got the florist's bill yesterday for Daddy's flowers from over there. Would you be able to find out from Aunt Amy who has the money? I don't want to let the bill go too long but don't particularly think I should have to pay it, either.

> *Blue ballpoint on heavy, pink-tinted stationery. The hand is a large unslanted cursive, sprawling from edge to edge of each page and deeply incised, actually perforating the paper in two places: the exclamation point in the second paragraph, and (in the postscript) the cross of the "t" in "particularly."*

41

## 2. *November 7, 1953*

Dear Mother –

That sounds like a good idea to make Tom an embalmer, for it's a sure thing he seems crazy about the work. I'm glad he and Wilma have patched it up. Maybe all this has helped them see how lucky they are to still have each other.

Speaking of helping, Mother, Hank would like very much to come back and work for you and help you with anything he could do. He thinks so much of you, Mother, and he wants to do this for you for nothing, because he would be so grateful for whatever spare time he might have for his writing. He has so little time to really work hard at it here, what with his full time job he needs to be able to afford our apartment. He had to go back to work for the government just for us to have enough to live on, and that doesn't make him any too happy. If we could live with you for a little while until we found a place close by that was reasonable, maybe I could get my old job back at NCR and bring us in some extra money.

I told him that you need him to do so many things like washing the cars, and helping on ambulance trips. I think for many years he felt that nobody needed or cared about him. Of course they worked him to death at that foster home when he was in high school but nobody there ever thanked him for it, or seemed to care about anything but the work getting done. It would be so wonderful for all of us. You would have someone to help day or night. Hank would have more time to write and what's the most important to me, we would all be together again.

Well, I better close and get to my washing.

All our love,

Phyllis and Hank

*Blue fountain pen on light green airmail stationery. Writing is small and precise, the lines of text perfectly straight, as if written with a sheet of lined paper underneath for a template. Wide, even margins on all four sides.*

3.  *November 24, 1953*

Dear Phyllis,

Please excuse typing and delay. Just starting with estate work for the court. Haven't had any jobs at all since Mrs. Glotfelter and that was paid before Daddy died. We had our hearse on a funeral for Coyne's and will get a little something for that. I see by the paper that we haven't lost any jobs yet, but we're bound to. I know some folks will not want a lady Funeral Director. They won't think we can handle it since Daddy is gone. I only hope everybody doesn't feel that way. I'm telling you this so you know what the situation is. I have been thinking very seriously about a lot of things. If you two would want to come back and stay here until we see how business is going to be, it will be okay with me. You're right, if Hank were here regular he could go on ambulance trips and drive the cars in addition to things around the house. With no-one here all the time I can't book all the vehicle use we might get other than our own jobs, and that income isn't to be laughed off. I don't expect he would care to learn embalming, or would he? Anyway, that's how it is. If you can decide to come back and are willing to take things as they come, then the sooner you can make it the better. Uncle Harold is moving in next week and I thought I would give him the big bedroom on the third floor that Edgar and the other apprentices used to use. You and Hank could have the bedroom you girls used to sleep in. Please excuse lack of paragraphs but as I have told you before paragraphs take up so much time and lose so much space typing I forget about them. Will ring off for this time and start supper.

Lots of love,
Mother

XXXXXXXXXXXXX

*Entire text (including the word "Mother" and the row of thirteen "X"'s) typewritten on brittle onionskin paper. Characters are faint, as if the ribbon were nearly dry. One error ("y" for "u" in "laughed") has been corrected by striking over.*

*Below the X's, a note in the same hand and pen as #2 above: "Movers — here at 10 tomorrow morn." Blank space beneath, a full third of the page.*

43

# RESPONSIBILITIES

12 February 1954

Dear Dana:

The Interminable Revenue "Service" sent us a cheery little note, which I enclose for your amazement. I also enclose a cheerful little telephone bill, likewise importuning us for payment. To speak bluntly, Dana, we don't have the dough to pay the goddam things… and would like, if possible, to borrow the funds from you.

Our financial situation is punk. Mildred, it turns out, is unable to pay us anything. Her take from insurance, which she thought was to be $250 per month, is actually $250 per quarter (or about $80 per month), and fails to even cover her own phone and ad bills. Business naturally slumped after Bob died. When it picks up again, we'll all be in a better position to sustain ourselves.

Phyllis did not land that part time job at NCR. She wound up with another one, though, at a newspaper office. She'll be bringing in about $20 a week.

I hate to go on about all this, Dana, but feel you should know why we are appealing for help yet again. Other bills are coming up, but we can handle those alright ourselves. Once we're over this income tax hump we'll be fine, and should even be able to save a cent or two after a couple of months.

I haven't produced any readable stuff yet. I'm up to my old trick of being super conscientious in all the wrong departments. I've cleaned this dump thoroughly from top to bottom, repaired all busted gadgets, and shoveled thousands of tons of snow. We've had three funerals since January 1, and because they were the first that Mildred ever had full responsibility for we worked our asses off on them. Mildred was in the spotlight, and her professional standing and whole business future depended on how these first funerals went over. Which they did, nicely. She is capable as hell, it turns out.

And now that we have a routine, a schedule, and know our individual roles on the team, I can switch my primary attention to writing. I am forced to conclude, after much going over and evaluating of events in my life thus far, that my tip-top peak experience was… selling ERRAND OF EXTERMINATION to *Esquire*.

And that the second-to-the-tip-top one was: having the blamed thing broadcast on TV.

Of course it wasn't the mere "selling" of our yarn that satisfied. We could "sell" cars, real estate, vacuum cleaners and other junk until the cows came home and not be in the least satisfied. But it turns out that <u>writing</u> itself – writing spanking-good stuff, <u>and</u> being published – are more fun than living backstage of a burlesque house.

As responsibilities go, that one is the pick of the litter.

(Hank)

*Typed (except signature) on green 8.5" x 11" paper. No errors.*

# SQUATTERS

February 1, 1955

Dear Dana:

Phyllis's sister and her family seem to have claimed squatters' rights here. They invade us practically every evening (five of them, if you count the goddam dog) – each competing earnestly for the title of World's Noisiest Human Being.

Their normal conversation is conducted in yells and bellows, and anyone else who wants to be heard has to match their decibel level. Phyllis and I, sitting inches apart, have to scream in order to carry on a conversation of our own. This is absolutely no exaggeration. These people haul their bedlam around with them like dirty underwear.

And when the house is under attack <u>all day</u> and rocking with din (which it usually is), you can imagine... the... condition... of ... my ... nerves.

Early morning (5 a.m.) is the <u>only</u> time to be <u>counted on</u> to be quiet enough for work. Unless, of course, the telephone rings and I'm out the door on an ambulance run. Or worse, the hearse. Different hat, same horse.

At least I've gotten my story-and-ideas files in order (they were a mess) and some things started. I expect to do a raft of science-fiction first off, some short and some long and some just plain silly. But production for sure – and in the stream of this production we may sift out a worthwhile piece here and there.

(Hank)

*Typed (except signature) on green 8.5" x 11" paper. No errors.*

# THE SOONER THE BETTER

Mar 25, '55

Dear Dana:

Small favor. Need ear plugs.

Badly.

Bedlam when Wilma and family here (practically all the time). Ear plugs unavailable in Dayton. Not a single one, let alone pair. Would you get a couple sets for me and send them on? I think I used to get them at Campbell's there on the corner of 14th and Decatur.

Sooner the better.

Thanks.

Hank

P.S.     5:30 a. m. Not typing this because might wake people up.

P.P.S.   Maybe I ought to wake everybody up. Show them the same consideration they show me when it comes to being quiet.

*Fine-point fountain-pen (indigo) on the same green 8.5" x 11" typing paper as above. Text spread evenly and sparsely across the entire sheet, clear margins all around.*

# POISON IVY

March 15, 1956

Dear Dana:

I've got poison ivy. Phyllis and I went fishing a week or so ago and I snatched out some weeds that were fouling our lines and got the itch. It's all over my right hand and makes typing awkward and writing with a pencil practically impossible. The junk the doctor gave me just seems to stimulate the itch to even greater activity.

Other irritations here are also worsening. Wilma's rabble, I mean. It's been pretty bad for a long time, with all of them constantly under foot and poisoning everything. We've put up with it because we hoped that in time they and Mildred would come to their senses and start conducting their lives like civilized human beings. That hardly seems possible now.

This is the way it is, as I see it – and I have no particular motive for telling you any of this, except to be able to get it off my chest.

Tom and Wilma both suffer from delayed infancy. They are self-centered and wanton in their raw desires, incapable of mature thought or judgment, totally irresponsible. I don't know why Tom is immature, but I presume it's for the same reason that Wilma is – because she was indulged in everything and allowed to do exactly as she pleased and never taught anything about being responsible for herself. Since Phyllis obviously was, I don't know how Wilma missed that schooling, but she did. And then she found someone who is exactly as helpless at coping with life, in even the most basic ways, as herself.

All of this would mean little to me, except that they camp in my tent and make my life, and the lives of everyone in the tent, miserable. Mildred permits the depredations without the slightest protest: pays their mortgage, gives them grocery money, allows them free run of the place here at their own unpredictable will. And she does so for a rather striking, though quite predictable, reason.

She has failed as a mother.

And she will avoid admitting a failure of such magnitude, at all costs.

Even the cost of sacrificing herself.

Or sacrificing others.

You see, to a woman being a successful mother is the most important thing there is. If she fails in that she fails in the central purpose of her existence. I can even sympathize, to a degree. Admitting

48

such a failure would be unbearable – like us admitting failure at writing.

But it's why you so often see the mothers of murderers and other criminals tenaciously defending their un-reared and hence socially deformed offspring and claiming beyond all reason that they are "good boys." They will do anything rather than shoulder the blame for the freaks of nurture they have produced.

And that is very clearly what is happening here.

You might reasonably wonder why we don't talk turkey to these delinquents, and straighten things out once and for all.

We don't for two reasons. One is that plain talk would only ignite the quick tempers of all of us and result in the immediate destruction of everything. The other reason, of course, is that none of these people are capable of listening, or of understanding anything they do not want to understand. The only time they <u>will</u> understand – and perhaps not even then – is when Phyllis and I eventually abandon them and the funeral business collapses and they all, including the parasites, founder and drown.

There is no consolation in knowing that nature will work its inexorable retribution, because the only desire I have is to get on with the work of writing – without interference, and in a spirit of good will.

I think, frankly, that it is partly because of this tortured situation that I was particularly sensitive to your criticism of my last batch of story drafts. It seems – or seemed – merely another unendurable obstruction. As though now every hand was against me and nothing that I attempted would ever be permitted to achieve its natural result.

This is the worst kind of frustration. But perhaps, as Carlyle said, a certain amount of misery is the lot of all of us, and we are to be tempered by it.

But Carlyle also said "Blessed is he who has found his work; let him ask no other blessedness."

I hope, Dana, that you don't mind serving as a wailing wall. I could go on at greater length, but even this much has been a relief. Phyllis and I pound each other's ears, but that has become to some extent almost like talking to ourselves. We need a bystander to growl at occasionally.

I still think things will work out – eventually. See remark on nature, above.

Of course, nature also gave us poison ivy.

Happy Ides of March....

Hank

*Typed (including sign-off) on green 8.5" x 11" paper. No errors.*

## MAKESHIFT V: *"An Errand of Extermination"*

In my father's *Esquire* story,
it turns out
the microbes WERE the Martians,
teeming in the flesh
of an anthropoid alien
so obviously comatose
it couldn't have piloted the vessel
it landed in.
                    Imagine bacteria
evolved enough to appear
as a multitude of brain-wave patterns
on the newly invented
electro-encephalograph
the army'd had shipped in from London.

Colonel Ward was intrigued. *It might,*
*he found himself thinking,*
*have been interesting*
*to hobnob with intelligent germs…*

But his stateside base
was quarantined, the fatal
flu-like symptoms spreading.
Alcoholic since his wife's death
some years earlier, he was relieved
to see the remedy arrive at last, although

*he didn't get to see much.*
*Only a sudden blinding glare,*
*then a hurricane of smoke*
*mushrooming up and out.*
*In a second, it was over.*

– Effective and eloquent
for a makeshift solution.

## WORK BOOK

My father's five-by-seven
three-ring binder – black,
with a Vermeer postcard
glued to the cover

(light, of course:
light
trembling on a girl's
moist under-lip).
                            Inside,
paper-clipped to the front page,
a dozen construction paper
squares, oblongs, ovoids,
a bit of typing on each:

> *ATTRACT* – *eye*
> *ear*
> *taste*
> *smell*

∽

> *HOW ABOUT THE OPPOSITE?*

∽

> *1. WHO?*
> *2. WHAT WANT?*
> *3. WHY want, WHY can't have?*
> *4. WHEN?*
> *5. WHERE?*
> *6. HOW achieve WANT?*

Pinholes in all of them.
Pulled off the wall, I suppose –
and in a hurry,
judging from the out-of-character
disorder: some turned upside-down,
some blank side up. The top one
stained with rust from the clip.

On the following pages,
cut to size
from 10-lb Blue Horse bond,
more typing:

> *Kelland – who wrote more than Dumas –*
> *chained himself to his desk every morning.*

> ⤜

> *The way to write is to write*
> *and write and write.*

At the back
a packet of store-bought notebook filler,
lined and ruled and brown with age,
still in its paper sleeve.
Too obvious to be a symbol,
too banal....

*Henry F. Guth*
*1919-1996*

# III. Conjectures

# THE WAY TO WRITE

*is to write and write and write*
but every evening,
half an hour after dinner,

there came Harold's
heavy tread on the third-
floor steps: that same

pause halfway up,
same hitched breath and
loud, bubbling fart....

a miracle, Hank thought,
of regularity. Next, as if on cue,
his two toddler nieces

scrabbling like puppies
at the bottom of the stairs.
He'd chased them off himself

(three times last week!)
but no one took the hint.
It wasn't HIS house.

൙

Pulps, he knew, were dying out.
The qualities still
bought short fiction –

mostly, these days,
from professors
and their well-trained students –

but the middle-market slicks, like *Esquire*,
that he'd finally broken into
just before his wedding

were turning more and more
to news, advice,
show-business gossip....

෴

Sometimes,
standing guard
in the doorway of his writing room

above the din of after-supper
cigarette-and-coffee talk,
he might, I imagine

have found himself
wishing for the business phone to ring,
for his mother-in-law

to holler up the stairs
about an ambulance run
that would bring

a brief release from unsuccess —
unasked-for, hence
resentable as interruption.

## ELVIS AND MY FATHER FAIL TO REACH AN ARTISTIC AGREEMENT

1.

A body pickup,
out to St. Elizabeth's and back.
Tom, in the passenger seat,
turns on the radio
(not asking Hank if he'd mind, of course)
and of course it's that Presley kid –
little more than half Hank's age
and trying it all in the home stretch
of a two-minute single:
veering from eerie
delta-blues falsetto
to gospel shiver to burbling
Bing and Dean. Too deep,
too high, too
close to the mike....
      For Christ's sake,
he's got no idea what he's doing,
throwing it all together like that:
like a taxi-dancing booth
at a church fund-raiser.


2.

Hank, at 36,
has little taste for the
"eclectic." Likes
a rulered line of ideal and
original action – simple,
unconflicted – in life
as well as art.
     Thus Darrell Bond,
rocket-pilot hero of his short story
"Planet in Reverse,"
abducting the delicate
Neptunian girl who'd kissed him
deeply, familiarly,
the first time he saw her
but who seemed,
as time went by, to cool off:

57

standing further and further from him,
talking with less
and less warmth in her
unintelligible tongue, until
the day she passed him by
with only a nervous glance.
                              Yet,
once removed from her planet's
retrograde time stream, her affections
(as Bond had calculated)
bloomed again. She smiled,
and so much more: her pretty lips made plain
and forward-moving English sense.


        3.
"Phyllis like this boy?" asks Tom.
"We heard him last week
on Looziana Hayride, and
swear to God, old Willie
like to bust the bed on me that night!"


Hank remembers
watching Tom watch –
avidly, it seemed – an embalmer
threading surgical suture
through a woman's nipples,
drawing her withered breasts
together into taut,
presentable peaks....


It's all a bad fit. What in the hell
does music have to do with sex
or sex with death? And why,
oh why, would they ever
put a radio in a goddam hearse?


        4.
He's got no answer.

# KENTUCKY RAIN

*Whatever the dreamer tells us must count as his dream. -- Freud*

For forty years,
my father swore his brother-in-law
tried to kill him one night

on the back roads
outside Beaver Lick, Kentucky.
They'd left Dayton after dinner,

with a body to deliver
for the Graham Funeral Home –
a three-hour night drive

up into the hills
on two-lane switchbacks
slick with rain and gravelly washout;

curves so tight
the hearse's back wheels floundered
off the fraying asphalt.

Straight there and back, though,
no services,
so they could sleep in the next day…

No, dammit,
there was a funeral at noon.
Hank knew

Tom would never think
to come over and help him
hose this night's worth of road-grit

off the car. It wasn't Tom
who lived at the funeral home;
it wasn't Tom

who washed and waxed the Meteor's
twenty feet of black lacquered steel
every Sunday it didn't rain;

who scrubbed its chrome snout
free of tar and bugs
with an old toothbrush.

"Who'll notice that?"
his mother-in-law had asked.
"We just need the sides and windows clean!"

So much for appreciation....
To be fair, he supposed,
Tom did have his hands full

steering his gas station into bankruptcy
and keeping Wilma pregnant.
Hank had heard her

making THAT announcement.
Right before they left, of course,
along with a plea to her mother

for more money. Yet this trip
was their first job in two weeks!
Where did they suppose

the cash would come from,
if Hank decided
he was sick of supporting all of them

with only a bed and meals
in return? Another sharp curve:
pumping the brakes,

Hank watched his high-beams
clear the tops of bare trees off to the right and
dissolve in the empty night air.

This far into the backwoods,
the maps he'd brought along were useless.
Tom seemed to know the way, though –

"Get up this rise here
and make your first left.
We're nearly 'bout there now."

Neither of them, I suppose,
could hear that thin, dry grinding noise
beneath the floorboards in the back.

What Hank did hear,
what he would remember ever after,
was that disembodied sound of hymns

rising like a beeswarm
out of the brambly ground around
a tipsy clapboard meeting house.

He'd remember that old
hill-jack preacher
standing in the doorway to greet them,

bald but for two stiff
wings of steel-grey hair
jutting straight up on each side of his head.

"It's our Wednesday night
prayer-meetin. We just
kep it a little bit late

and made a visitation supper
outen the deal.
You boys'll join us, won't you?"

The platters of fat ribs,
washed with sugar and cider vinegar,
will also linger in his memory

along with the thick black coffee
and slices of whiskey pie
(had he heard that right?);

the raw stone walls of the church-cellar
glittering with seepage,
punctured here and there

by crooked fingers of roots;
that long, long blessing
over the food, some kind of

call and response
the entire congregation seemed
to perform in perfect unison –

even the widowed husband
and his motherless children.
Even Tom....

"Yea, all are welcome" –
*"Yes, Lord"* –
"all are bidden" – *"hear Him now"* –

"to this FEAST of the Lord" –
*"Yes"* – "Him who giveth" –
*"Yes, He giveth"* –

"Yea,
 I say who GIVETH" –
*"Praise Him, He giveth"* –

"and Who" – *"Yes, Lord,
 yes, we know You"* –
"taketh away…"

 Suddenly queasy from the noise,
 the heat, the fumes
 from that chattering gas-powered generator

tucked away in a corner,
Hank yelled to Tom
"I'm going to lie down for awhile.

Start back whenever you're ready –
if I'm asleep,
don't wake me up."

&

I want to think
that, as he settled himself
on the stiff cold vinyl

of the gurney mattress,
Hank felt a twinge of worry
for Phyllis. Had she tried

to go to sleep yet? Had she
gotten up again,
as she'd been doing

nearly every night
for the past year
since her father died,

to wait for daylight somewhere –
anywhere – else in the house?
Perhaps he recalled

that morning her mother found her
asleep in one of the kitchen chairs,
the squares of black and white linoleum

beneath her bare feet
covered with drying blood and milk
and broken glass.

He might have had
and then rejected
the thought that she was getting

worse, not better – if only
to help him
swallow down his own frustration

(no, his fear)
that bringing her back to her parents' house
had been a mistake,

although it was what she'd wanted
in those first weeks
after losing her father.

How do you explain
where you end up? How
do you distribute blame?

That blame must be assigned
was obvious. For every obstacle,
for every wasted breath or motion,

each and any diminishment in life,
there was fault: identifiable,
not his....

&

Scutter of gravel. The vast
ass-end of the hearse
fishtailing, shaking him

bonelessly on the flimsy
collapsible litter.
Underneath him, metal

screamed and snapped
the tail-gate
was flopping open he

was rolling toward it
grabbing at the curtains feet
out over empty

air
then back in
as the hurtling weight pitched

slowly up and forward
and finally back down,
crunching to a halt

on that cold Kentucky back-road,
in the drizzling rain
of a dead November pre-dawn.

Trembling, panting,
he reached for the flashlight
he'd thought to stow in the tire-well.

Felt a broad hand
fall on his shoulder, then
lift as he turned,

his elbow lunging at Tom's throat.
"Whoa, Nelly...."
Palms up, Tom

backed slowly away.
How DO you explain
where you end up?

Hank knew he'd latched that gate;
he'd even double-checked it. He knew that.
Caught in the flashlight beam,

his brother-in-law's face
hovered before him: the low, dark brow,
the rounded jowls, a boxer's

pulpy nose. But why...?
Because he could,
of course. What other reason

did there need to be?
Hank shifted his light
to the hearse's empty

left rear fender: shreds of tire
wedged beneath the bumper.
From the rear, like squashed guts,

trailed the burned-out differential
and an axle. "Hot damn!"
shouted Tom, from a distance.

"Turn that flash-beam
thisaway!" Hank did—
and saw, a good hundred feet back,

the gurney he'd been sleeping on
hung upside-down
in a tumbled wire fence. Above it,

the black night sky was slowly
turning a sodden,
back-lit grey. "Hot damn!"

Tom said again.
"Ain't you the lucky one?"
Hank shook his head, amazed.

This couldn't be his life.

## DEDICATION

It started with those oddball names
in his new wife's family:
Zilpha, Mellie,

Vernie and Norval, Ora, Hoyt....
Pump-priming, he'd called it.
You never knew,

he told his son years
later, what
might make the imagination

catch, turn over,
idle into life. And so,
his magnum opus:

three thick loose-leaf notebooks
holding, by his own count, some
nine thousand

seven hundred thirteen entries
harvested from memory,
from phonebooks, the newspaper,

the dead in the mortuary
downstairs. Alphabetized
and typed in double columns

(black for male, red for female),
the entire collection
organized by national origin,

each country picked out
with its own hand-printed label
on a self-adhesive celluloid tab.

All work
and no play
could make Hank a dull boy.

# IV. Truths

# THE PERSISTENCE OF MEMORY

According to my father,
Bob Graham was barely cold
before his widow, my grandmother,
had her whole back yard –

lawn, flagstone path,
a pretty little cherry tree – torn out
to make room for a parking lot. And then,
compounding this disgrace,

replaced the piano
in her downstairs front hall
(the one my mother had taken lessons on)
with an electric organ just for funerals.

I knew, of course,
that for the twenty-three years
she survived him, Grandma
had kept Bob's name, not hers,

in the Dayton telephone directory.
Had put clean sheets
on both twin beds each week. Had
left that 1953 motor-club calendar

on the wall
between their matching headboards –
open to October, always,
and a blaze of orange and scarlet leaves

at each end of a covered bridge somewhere.
I could see it,
even in the dark,
from my cot against the far wall

on those nights I stayed over
and fell asleep while lights flowed
back and forth across the ceiling
from a few cars on the street below.

It's as if her grief,
like some strange
night-blooming flower, has
revived again,

surviving in these memories
of her stubborn, mixed ambitions:
half going on, half
laboring against herself

to stop time —

# UNSAID: THEME AND VARIATIONS

*From a letter (my father to his future in-laws, 29 November 1951):*

It's probably obvious that I think highly of Phyllis. In fact, I love her.
Easy to say… but love's a complicated emotion. I don't exactly worship
her, or anyone else for that matter, or ever expect to boost her up to the
chilly top of a pedestal where she would perish of boredom (a dirty trick
to play on any woman). But I've always been a man, and intend to
continue as one, and feel about her in that way. I would do practically
anything for her, short of violating immutable principles of God that I
believe in or turning myself into a spineless caricature of a man. A
precept of Jesus', "what is a man profited if he shall gain the whole
world and lose his own soul?" is hard to beat as sound philosophy.


    1.
I want you to think well of me,
but it's my business – our business,
Phyllis's and mine – what time of day or night
we choose to travel. We could, you know,
have stopped halfway to Dayton,
shacked up in some motel
and rolled into town at noon the next day.
What you need to understand,
without my saying it, is this:
I do not care
what you or your flashlight-wielding neighbors
think. And none of your fears
about some stain on that fine cloak of respectability
you wrap your funeral business in, will ever –
not now, not at any point in the future –
interfere in any plans I make with Phyllis.
There will be no more of this
horse-shit by mail,
haranguing her for "driving all night with a man."


    2.
Let me start again.
            I know
what your real worry is
                    but I can't be the one

to bring the subject up.
                        And yet,
since I'm a stranger to you,
                        you can't broach it either.
The plain fact, though,
                        as you must see for yourselves,
is that Phyllis simply
                        isn't like her sister.
Nor am I like Tom.
                        And what we have together
(though I'm damned if I know
                        how to prove it to you)
isn't simply that
                hormonal combustion
camouflaged for centuries
                        by flatulent songwriters
and sophomoric poets
                        (even Shakespeare, I'm afraid)
as "worship."
                Worship, I submit, is immature,
emotionally and sexually.
                        I do not worship Phyllis.


        3.
So how can I,
a man full-grown
and writing to the parents
of the woman he knows is his —

how can I demonstrate
that what I'll give her
(and what I need from her as well)
is that same

bone-deep understanding
I observed between the two of you?
It would be condescending of me
to report that I watched you

74

walking side by side to church
that Sunday morning of our visit.
That I studied
the way you stepped together,

holding hands,
around that broken sidewalk slab:
never missing a stride,
never splitting apart

nor jostling one another,
each of you
knowing so well which
way the other one would move

that you could pass the obstacle
united. How to tell you that –
except, perhaps,
to mention it to Phyllis?

4.
You need to know
that I know love's as real

and necessary,
and in the same way,

as a hot meal when you're hungry.
If you've ever gone without (and I have),

then you'll know how hard it is
to ask for sustenance.

But you don't turn it down
when it's offered. Not

if you want to live. I'm sorry
Tom and Wilma separated.

I'm sorry for their baby. You have worries;
I'm not one of them.

5.  Mark 8:36

*For what shall it profit a man,*
*if he shall gain the whole world,*
*and lose his own soul?*

I told you
I don't worship Phyllis.
I don't worship Jesus, either,

but he said some fine things.
Being a writer,
I lay claim to all of human thought

that seems worthwhile. And
like that man
you go to church to believe in,

I don't have much use
for property or social standing.
But my guess is

you'll be pleased enough
just seeing his holy name
that his ideas won't fully register. Oh well,

I'll know they're there.
I didn't say
I was quoting from memory,

but you're welcome
to think so. The problem
was those "Shalls" –

just too close together –
so I touched the passage up
a little bit.

# HOME TRUTHS

*O earth, cover not thou my blood, and let my cry have no place. -- Job 16:18*

*What's left to examine*
*after the memories, letters, photographs?*

*My grandparents' wills.*
*Estate tax forms on microfilm.*
*Some mortgage documents.*

*A few old friends of theirs*
*still living. My grandfather's last apprentice*
*who last worked for him sixty years ago.*
*But the living only know so much*

*and the dead, of course,*
*don't speak.*
        *Shall I*
*speak for her? Shall I*
*try to explain?*

    1.
Wilma was my daughter.
Them girls were my grandkids.
What in the Sam Hill was I supposed to do?
I wasn't going to let them starve in the street!

    2.
I guess you figured out by now
I wasn't as well-off as your Dad
was always saying I was. See,
paying cash for that new hearse
put-near cleaned out our savings,
so your grandpa made another note on the house
to give us back some cash. He never liked
to borrow money on a car, you know –
the value don't hold up. He figured
he could get the cost back, though,
by renting it out to other funeral homes.

It WAS about the finest hearse in town
there for awhile.
                    But see,
now Coyne was about the only one
who'd still have anything to do with us.
Your grandpa never wanted to admit it,
but that Hawley business... well,
it really put a crimp in us.
Your father never knew about it,
so I'm glad you found out. It'll help you
see what we was up against.


        3.
It's just like Edgar told you:
Hawley's contract with the VA hospital
was only on the veterans themselves. Nobody else.
"Supply transport of remains, and/or embalming services"
for such and such an amount....
I used to have the whole darn thing by heart.
                                    But yes,
it was a nurse out there that died
while Hawley was having his operation
and we was on call for the contract work.
So when the family asked us if we'd do HER funeral,
of course we said yes.
Must have been the VA give our name out –
we sure didn't contact them!
                        And oh,
Jed Hawley nearly went up!
Accused us both of stealing his business,
said we owed him everything
we made on that job. Tell you what,
we probably WOULD have give him half,
to keep the peace. But when he started talking like that?
well, your grandpa and I both dug our heels in.
And THAT'S when he went griping
to the Funeral Directors' Association.
He was thick as thieves with most of them, of course.
And he was a bigger outfit than we were,
so when we said we wasn't going to pay him
one red cent no matter what,
they voted us right out. And then –

well, we was just like poison
to every other funeral home in town.

Well yes, except for Coyne.
But wasn't like he done us any favors.
All's we ever got from him was overload,
from when he booked more funerals or medicals
than he had vehicles for.
                      I know, I know,
old Edgar always did think
they was helping us out. But Coyne,
his whole thing was to build HIMSELF up.
So he wouldn't just refer a call – oh no,
he didn't want us getting OUR name
out there for service. No,
we always had to look like HIS employees.
Your father told you, didn't he, how they made him
take our nameplate out of our car's window
when we went out on a job for them?
And wouldn't even let us bill directly!
Paid us himself, he did,
and set his own damn piddling rates, too!

But he did help keep us alive
that first year after your grandpa died.
It seemed like we was losing all our families
from the church and lodges. I kept up my dues
with Eastern Star, of course. But then
I couldn't get out to functions like I could
when there was both of us,
'cause somebody had to stay there for the phone.
That's why nobody you were talking to
remembered much about me
after your grandpa was gone.
I couldn't afford an answering service
and your mom and dad, they liked to go out
after he stopped doing his writing in the evening.
I got Unk to watch the phone a couple times,
but then he actually got a call once
and they thought he was –

well –

79

a little slow. You never know
how things like that are gonna get around,
and we didn't need no more to worry about.
So I just started staying in.
                              Your grandpa, now,
he kept in with the Masons and the Shrine.
And what with all that Hawley mess,
he even joined the Ancient Order of Druids
to try and build up contacts. After he died, though,
that all pretty much dried up.
I got your Dad to join the Masons,
but he never would go out to meetings –
only those McAdams nights, when they had movies.


        4.
I know you want to know about him and me.
Well, tell you what:
I don't think anybody in the family
ever had the straight of that one. I sure didn't.
All's I know is that your father and his writing
weren't the most important things going on
when he and your mother were staying with me.
Not if he wasn't making money off it. Land's sake,
I knew he didn't care for funeral work.
I wasn't all that wild about it myself,
if anybody wants to know. But it was what I had.
And it was paying the bills, at least.


And we did need him. It helped
just having him there: somebody who could go to work
whenever we got work. Right after your grandpa died,
it was harder'n hell sometimes
to find a man or two to go out on an ambulance call.
I didn't see no sense paying full-time help
to sit around and wait for business.


        5.
You did know about your mother, didn't you?
How bad she was
when they first moved back in?

80

I never in all my born days
saw a body grieve so hard. She looked...
she looked sick, tell you the honest truth.
Her mouth was pinched up,
like she had pain somewhere...
I was afraid for awhile it might be cancer!
Even had that musty smell sick people get.
I wondered once or twice if maybe your dad...

but he wasn't.
Hurting her, I mean. I just...

I didn't know what to think there for awhile.

6.

I'll tell you this:
I always did believe them coming back
was her idea. Even though she SAID
it was him that offered.
                        And you have to realize:
all's I had was what your grandpa left me.
If I'd closed the business, sold the house and cars,
I could have lived a few years on the cash,
but then what? I was only forty-six.
I even had to pay the state inheritance tax
to go on living in my own house! Then,
to top it off, there come that letter
from the stinking County Probate Court
about "concealing assets."
                        Well,
you saw the papers. What I done was,
when your grandpa died, I took
nine hundred and fourteen dollars off the figure
I told them was in our savings account.
See, that was money from MY mother
when SHE died. And we only got it
a couple-few months before your grandpa passed away
(it never rains but what it pours!).
And since we'd paid tax on it once already,
I couldn't see being skinned again.

But then, of course,
they had to have some kind of affidavit
from my lawyer to verify it.
Then HE turned around
and charged put-near as much
as what I would have paid in extra taxes!

     7.

I know what your father thought about me.
How my husband had just died
and all's I had was money on my mind.
Well, tell you what: the world
don't give you very long to mourn a loss.
And while you're doing it, you got to eat.
That's why I took your dad's help.
Even if I'd known how things was going to end up,
I don't think I could have done no different
and kept on living.

    ⁊

*My grandmother's kitchen: the table, as usual,*
*cluttered with cups and plates, prescription bottles,*
*the stack of morning-paper comics*
*she'd saved out for me.*
                *"Know what?" she asks.*
                              *I do,*
*but that's not how the game goes.*
                      *"No, what?"*
*"Grandma loves you!"*

                                           *Mildred Daganhardt Graham*
                                          *1907-1977*

# THE UNDERTAKER'S WIDOW
*October 8, 1953*

They phoned her at breakfast: he'd begun to fail.
Still, it was dark before she got back home
and scraped the shrivelled egg-yolk, waxy and pale,
off her plate; turned out the kitchen light.
                                    The gloom,
the whine of a late bus coasting to their curb,
reminded her of getting up for night calls.
Not needing lights, or talk that might disturb
their sleeping girls (both married now), he'd pause

just long enough to drink the Coke she'd poured
or smoke a Lucky, while they sat together
around a corner of the table: absorbed,
like the air they breathed, into each other. Beneath her

     *(his heart attack was just ten days ago!)*

the floor rolled once. And that would have to do.

## FARMER'S DAUGHTER
*1928*

Millie Daganhardt, her parents' last-born,
was sure at twenty who she wanted: Bob Graham,
ten years older, and divorced besides!

She'd heard the talk at church, about a child
somebody'd overheard somebody else
claim to have seen him with. But none of them
could even say if it was a boy or girl.
The wife, they thought, was living over in Troy.

There was no child. Mildred knew, because
she'd gone to Bob and asked him, and he'd said so.
Wasn't angry, either – understood
that, since it had come up in public, she'd need
to ask him again. She'd need to be sure.
                                        Meanwhile,
her parents saw him steady at his trade,
not just his courting, and (although his past
was cause for worry) said that, if he asked,
they'd sign the marriage license.
                                Which is why,
the story goes, she went down to the courthouse
one day AFTER her twenty-first birthday.

The thing was, she'd have taken him child or no.
But, as he'd pointed out in his own case,
you couldn't prove what hadn't happened. Therefore,
she would do what could be done: make known,
to all concerned, that her consent to him
was hers, and hers alone – not underwritten
by any other name at church or law.
She'd give him that, like a gift she'd saved up for.

My mother was born nine months and eight days later.

# FAMILY ROMANCE

### 1.

This is the story my mother told.
Still mourning for her father after two years,
she could barely speak yet; barely ate,
hardly slept. But then, as she lay in the dark
in that last full moment of her grief,
he was there: his long white robe
like a light at the foot of the bed,
his face as she had known it, his voice
telling her not to worry any longer. Telling her
"I've just been made an angel."
                                    From that night,
she knew she could continue with her life.

### 2.

This is what my father might have said,
but never did. That they'd been married
less than thirteen months when her father died.
That they were sleeping in her childhood bedroom.
That he lay beside her every night
and saw no robes, no angels – only
the dark pool of a mirror on the wall,
bookshelves he'd built himself, lights
flowing back and forth across the ceiling
from a few cars on the street below.
                                    That he loved her –
and that that had made no difference to her grief.

*West Chester, Pennsylvania – Cincinnati, Ohio – Jackson, Tennessee*
*(1995-2005, 2017)*

# SOURCES

Althoff, Shirley. Personal interview. 6 July 2000.

Althoff, William. Personal interview. 6 July 2000.

Bauer, Brad (Special Collections Librarian). *Joseph W. Roberts Collection of Scripts for Television, 1951-1952*. Special Collections Holdings Descriptions, The American Archive of Broadcasting. N.d. <http://www.tol.lib.ca.us/1spcolde.html>.

Bowman, Eva. Letter to Robert C. Graham and Mildred D. Graham. 1 Sept. 1953. Author's collection.

---. Letter to Robert C. Graham and Mildred D. Graham. 4 Sept. 1953. Author's collection.

Brewer, Brenda. "Mea culpa, mea culpa, mea culpa." E-mail to the author. 4 Sep. 2000.

Daganhardt, Mary M. Letter to Phyllis J. Graham. 7 June 1951. Author's collection.

Department of Public Welfare, Division of Health, Dayton, Ohio. Certificate of Death. Robert C. Graham, deceased. No. 48144A. 10 Oct. 1953. Author's collection.

Gem City Building and Loan Association of Dayton, Ohio. Mortgage. Robert C. Graham and Mildred D. Graham, mortgagors. Loan No. 3461. 26 Oct. 1951. Recorded in Montgomery County, Ohio, 27 Oct. 1951: Book No. 1362, Page 13. Author's collection.

Gem City Savings Association of Dayton, Ohio. Mortgage. Mildred D. Graham (widow), mortgagor. Loan No. 1503. 6 May 1960. Recorded in Montgomery County, Ohio, 6 May 1960: Book No. 1997, Page 719. Author's collection.

Graham, Mildred D., in living room, 1850 Wayne Ave., Dayton, Ohio. Personal photograph by unknown photographer. N.d. Author's collection.

Graham, Mildred D. and 1951 Cadillac Meteor, 1850 Wayne Ave., Dayton, Ohio. Personal photograph by unknown photographer. Apr. 1954. Author's collection.

Graham, Mildred D., and Robert C. Graham, in living room,1850 Wayne Ave., Dayton, Ohio. Personal photograph by unknown photographer. Author's collection.

Graham, Mildred D. Letter to Phyllis J. Graham. 2 Aug. 1943. Author's collection.

---. Letter to Phyllis J. Graham. 10 Aug. 1944. Author's collection.

---. Letter to Phyllis J. Graham. 31 Aug. 1951. Author's collection.

---. Letter to Phyllis J. Graham. 18 Oct. 1951. Author's collection.

---. Letter to Phyllis J. Graham. 17 Aug. 1952. Author's collection.

---. Letter to Phyllis J. Guth (neé Graham) and Henry F. Guth. 10 Oct. 1952. Author's collection.

---. Letter to Phyllis J. Guth (neé Graham) and Henry F. Guth. 9 Nov. 1952. Author's collection.

---. Letter to Phyllis J. Guth (neé Graham) and Henry F. Guth. 12 Feb. 1953. Author's collection.

---. Letter to Phyllis J. Guth (neé Graham) and Henry F. Guth. 12 Mar. 1953. Author's collection.

---. Letter to Phyllis J. Guth (neé Graham) and Henry F. Guth. 7 July 1953. Author's collection.

---. Letter to Phyllis J. Guth (neé Graham) and Henry F. Guth. 31 July 1953. Author's collection.

---. Letter to Phyllis J. Guth (neé Graham) and Henry F. Guth. 1 Nov. 1953. Author's collection.

---. Letter to Phyllis J. Guth (neé Graham) and Henry F. Guth. 24 Nov. 1953. Author's collection.

---. Letter to Phyllis J. Graham and Wilma Elaine Graham. 9 Aug. 1944. Author's collection.

Graham, Phyllis. "Class Song – 1947." Arr. A. Edwards. Unpublished manuscript. Author's collection.

Graham, Robert C., in kitchen, 1850 Wayne Ave., Dayton, Ohio. Personal photograph by unknown photographer. Dec. 1952. Author's collection.

Graham, Robert C. Letter to Phyllis J. Graham. 4 May 1949. Author's collection.

---. Letter to Phyllis J. Graham. 19 Oct. 1951. Author's collection.

---. Letter to Phyllis J. Guth (neé Graham) and Henry F. Guth. 7 July 1953. Author's collection.

---. Letter to Phyllis J. Guth (neé Graham) and Henry F. Guth. 31 July 1953. Author's collection.

Groven Company. Personal Property Mortgage. Mildred N. Graham and Robert C. Graham, mortgagors. 26 Sep. 1931. Recorded in Miami County, Ohio, 13 Oct. 1931. Author's collection.

Guth, Catherine. Personal interview. 18 Aug. 2000.

Guth, Henry and Mildred D. Graham, Woodland Cemetery, Dayton, Ohio. Personal photograph by Phyllis J.Guth. Apr. 1954. Author's collection.

Guth, Henry and Phyllis Guth, 1850 Wayne Ave., Dayton, Ohio. Personal photograph by Mildred D.Graham. Apr. 1954. Author's collection.

Guth, Henry. "An Errand of Extermination." *Esquire* Apr. 1952. 53+.

---. "Baby Diaper Man!" Unpublished manuscript with hand emendations. Author's collection.

---. "Bobo." Unpublished manuscript. Author's collection.

---. "Characters." Unpublished manuscript. Author's collection.

---. "Doom Ship." *Super Science Stories*. Nov. 1950. 86-94. Rpt. in *An Argosy Special: Science Fiction*. Ed. Lou Sahadi. New York: Popular Publications, 1977. 31+.

---. "Earthbound." *Planet Stories* 3.9 (Winter 1947): 84-89.

---. "The Outsider." Unpublished manuscript. Author's collection.

---. "Planet in Reverse." *Planet Stories* 3.10 (Spring 1948): 59-67.

---. *Pop and the Kid*. Unpublished manuscript. Author's collection.

---. "Popular Magazine   August, 1950   PERSONALS." Unpublished manuscript. Author's collection.

---. "The Renoir." Unpublished manuscript with hand emendations. Author's collection.

---. "Retribution." Unpublished manuscript. Author's collection.

---. "Signal Red." *Planet Stories* 4.4 (Fall 1949): 69-74.

---. "Strange Missile." Manuscript of text published as "An Errand of Extermination." Author's collection.

---. "The Terrible Atom Bomb." Unpublished manuscript. Author's collection.

---. "You're Going to Help Me." Unpublished manuscript. Author's collection.

---. Letter to Phyllis J. Graham. 30 Jan. 1952. Author's collection.

---. Letter to Phyllis J. Graham. 6 Feb. 1952. Author's collection.

---. Letter to Phyllis J. Graham. 12 Feb. 1952. Author's collection.

---. Letter to Phyllis J. Graham. 18 Feb. 1952. Author's collection.

---. Letter to Phyllis J. Graham. 28 Feb. 1952. Author's collection.

---. Letter to Phyllis J. Graham. 4 Mar. 1952. Author's collection.

---. Letter to Phyllis J. Graham. 27 Mar. 1952. Author's collection.

---. Letter to Phyllis J. Graham. 14 May 1952. Author's collection.

---. Letter to Phyllis J. Graham. 2 June 1952. Author's collection.

---. Letter to Robert C. Graham and Mildred D. Graham. 29 Nov. 1951. Author's collection.

---. Letter to Phyllis J. Guth (nee Graham). 1 Oct. 1953. Author's collection.

---. Letter to Phyllis J. Guth (nee Graham). 16 Oct. 1953. Author's collection.

---. Letter to Phyllis J. Guth (nee Graham). 20 Oct. 1953. Author's collection.

---. Letter to Dana W. Stockbridge. 12 Feb. 1954. Author's collection.

---. Letter to Dana W. Stockbridge. 25 Jan. 1955. Author's collection.

---. Letter to Dana W. Stockbridge. 1 Feb. 1955. Author's collection.

---. Letter to Dana W. Stockbridge. 12 Mar. 1956. Author's collection.

Guth, Phyllis J. (neé Graham). Letter to Mildred D. Graham. 9 Nov. 1953. Author's collection.

---. Letter to Robert C. Graham and Mildred D. Graham. 11 Sep. 1947. Author's collection.

---. Letter to Henry Guth. 27 Jan. 1952. Author's collection.

---. Letter to Henry Guth. 19 Feb. 1952. Author's collection.

---. Letter to Henry Guth. 30 Mar. 1952. Author's collection.

Hammond, Alfred S. Letter to Mildred D. Graham, 10 Apr. 1961. Author's collection.

*The History of Miami County, Ohio.* Chicago: W.H. Beers, 1880.

Junior League of Dayton, Ohio, Inc. *Dayton: A History in Photographs.* Intro. Allan W. Eckert. Dayton: Junior League of Dayton, Ohio, Inc. 1976.

Kennedy, David. "Business and tax records." E-mail to the author. 22 June 2000.

Kier, Vivian. Personal interview. 21 July 2000.

Kitchen, 1850 Wayne Ave, Dayton, Ohio. Personal photograph by unknown photographer. Dec. 1952. Author's collection.

McPherson, Thomas A. *American Funeral Cars and Ambulances Since 1900.* Glen Ellyn: Crestline, 1973.

Meredith, Scott. *Writing to Sell.* New York: Harper, 1950. Copy owned by Henry Guth, containing his marginal annotations and indexing. Author's collection.

"Mildred Graham rites held; ran funeral home." *Dayton Daily News,* n.d. (Feb. 1977).

Miller, Larry. *Ohio Place Names.* Bloomington: U Indiana P, 1996.

"Miss William [sic] Elaine Graham's engagement..." *Dayton Daily News,* n.d. (June 1950?).

Morton, Alan. *The Complete Directory to Science Fiction, Fantasy and Horror Television Series: A Comprehensive Guide to the First 50 Years, 1946- 1996.* Peoria: Other World Books, 1997.

---. Letter to the author. 6 Sep. 2000.

Moyer, Juda (Archivist, Troy Historical Society). Letter to the author. 25 Feb. 1997.

Office (Henry F. Guth), 1850 Wayne Ave., Dayton, Ohio. Personal photograph by unknown photographer (Henry F. Guth?). Author's collection.

"Phyllis Graham, Henry F. Guth Are Married, Take Trip South." *Dayton Daily News,* 21 Sept. 1952.

"Plague from Space." *Tales of Tomorrow*. By Mann Rubin (adapted from Henry Guth, "An Errand of Extermination"). Perf. Gene Raymond, Charles Proctor, Philip Pine, and Harry Landers.ABC. New York. 25 Apr. 1952.

Probate Court of Montgomery County, Ohio. Estate of Mary M. Daganhardt, deceased 29 Oct. 1952. Case No. 124124, Docket 120.

---. Estate of Mildred D. Graham, deceased 11 Feb. 1977. Case No. 218032, Docket 266.

---. Estate of Robert C. Graham, deceased 8 Oct. 1953. Case No. 127156, Docket 124.

Rabbitt, Eddie, and D. Heard. "Kentucky Rain." Perf. Elvis Presley 19 Feb. 1969. *Suspicious Minds: The Memphis 1969 Anthology.* RCA, 1999.

"R.C. Graham, City Funeral Director, Dies." *Dayton Daily News,* n.d. (Oct. 1953).

Robbins, Ross. Personal interview. 21 July 2000.

Saunders, Yann. "1951 Cadillac Meteor – combination hearse and ambulance." E-mail to the author. 16 Sep. 1998.

---. "1951 Cadillac Meteor." E-mail to the author. 15 June 2001.

---. "1955 Cadillac limousine." E-mail to the author. 26 June 2000.

Sieber, Mary, and Ken Buttolph. *Standard Catalogue of Cadillac, 1903-1990.* Iola, WI: Krause, 1991.

Singleton, C., and R.M. McCoy. "Trying to Get to You." Perf. Elvis Presley. Jul. 1955. *The Sun Sessions CD.* RCA, 1987.

Social Security Administration (unnamed customer service representative). Telephone interview. 17 July 2000.

State of Ohio, Miami County. Marriage License. Robert Chester Graham and Mildred Naomi Daganhardt. 7 Sept. 1928. Author's collection.

Stinson, John D. *Popular Publications, Inc. Records, c. 1910-1995.* New York Public Library, Manuscripts and Archives Division. April 1998. <http://www.nypl.org/research/chss/spe/rbk/faids/popular.html>.

Stockbridge, Dana. Letter to the author. 19 Jan. 1997.

---. Letter to the author. 24 Jan. 1997.

---. Telephone interview. 29 Oct. 2000.

---. Telephone interview. 9 June 2001.

Toolis, Lorna. "Merril Collection/Henry Guth." E-mail to the author. 1 Aug. 2000.

Washington Federal Savings and Loan Association of Dayton.
Mortgage Deed. Robert C. Graham and Mildred D. Graham,
Mortgagors. Loan No. 6320. 10 Dec. 1940. Recorded in
Montgomery County, Ohio, 13 Dec. 1940: Book No. 836,
Page 516. Author's collection.

Waterall, Robert. Telephone interview. 17 Sep. 2000.

Winters National Bank and Trust Company of Dayton. Chattel
Mortgage. Mildred D. Graham, Mortgagor. 5 Feb. 1960.
Recorded in Montgomery County, Ohio 24 Feb. 1960: Title No.
1286948. Author's collection.

---. Sixty-Day Loan. Graham Funeral Home: Mildred D. Graham, maker.
Loan No. 1917. 7 July 1964. Author's collection.

---. Sixty-Day Loan. Graham Funeral Home: Mildred D. Graham, maker.
Loan No. 4643. 6 Apr. 1967. Author's collection.

---. Sixty-Day Loan. Graham Funeral Home: Mildred D. Graham, maker.
Loan No. 7621. 25 July 1967. Author's collection.

LUMMOX Press

# BODY *and* SOUL

By Ryan Guth

"From its arresting beginning to its
startling end, *Body and Soul* mines
the rich ground where narrative and lyric
overlap. Ryan Guth makes us believe in
and feel for Cassandra Hart, whom life
has broken into multiple personalities,
weaving the many threads of her
persona—her grit, her fierceness, her

# Also by TRANSCENDENT ZERO PRESS

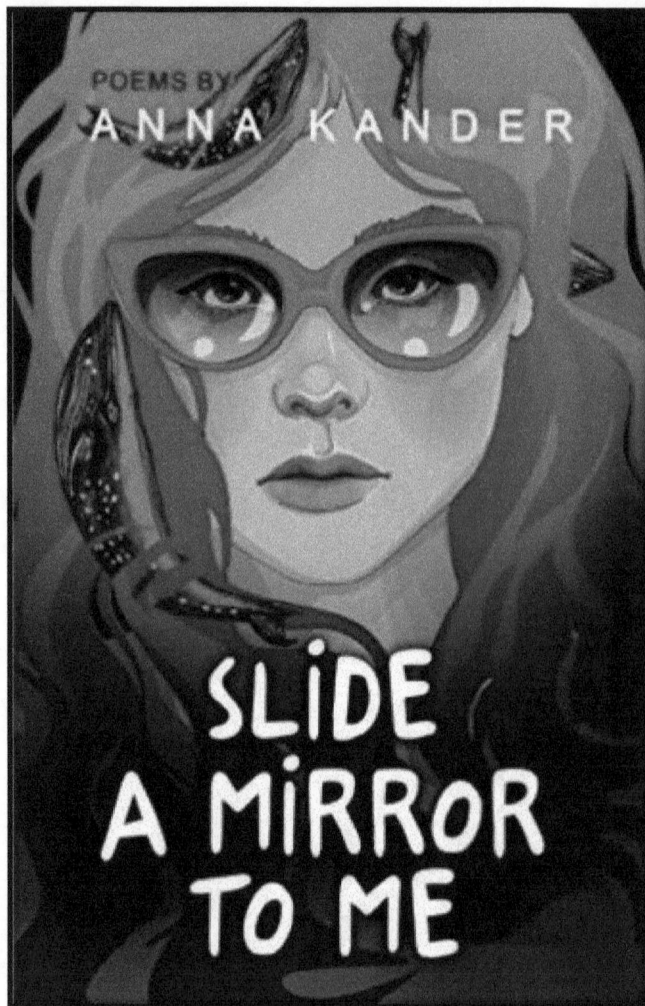

POEMS BY
ANNA KANDER

SLIDE
A MIRROR
TO ME

While training as a psychotherapist, a young woman recovering from anxiety is called to counsel a girl who's attempted suicide. Each must find a way to carry herself forward...

*Slide a Mirror to Me* is the debut poetry collection by Anna Kander, a Pushcart Prize-nominated author who previously trained as a psychotherapist. Kander weaves poems and stories into a loose narrative with villains, heroes, and hope.

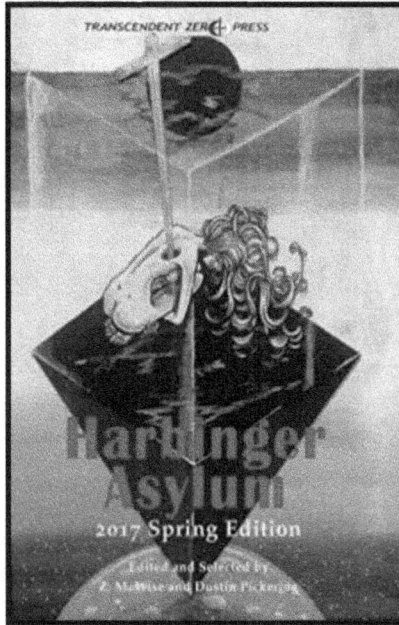

# Also by TRANSCENDENT ZERO PRESS

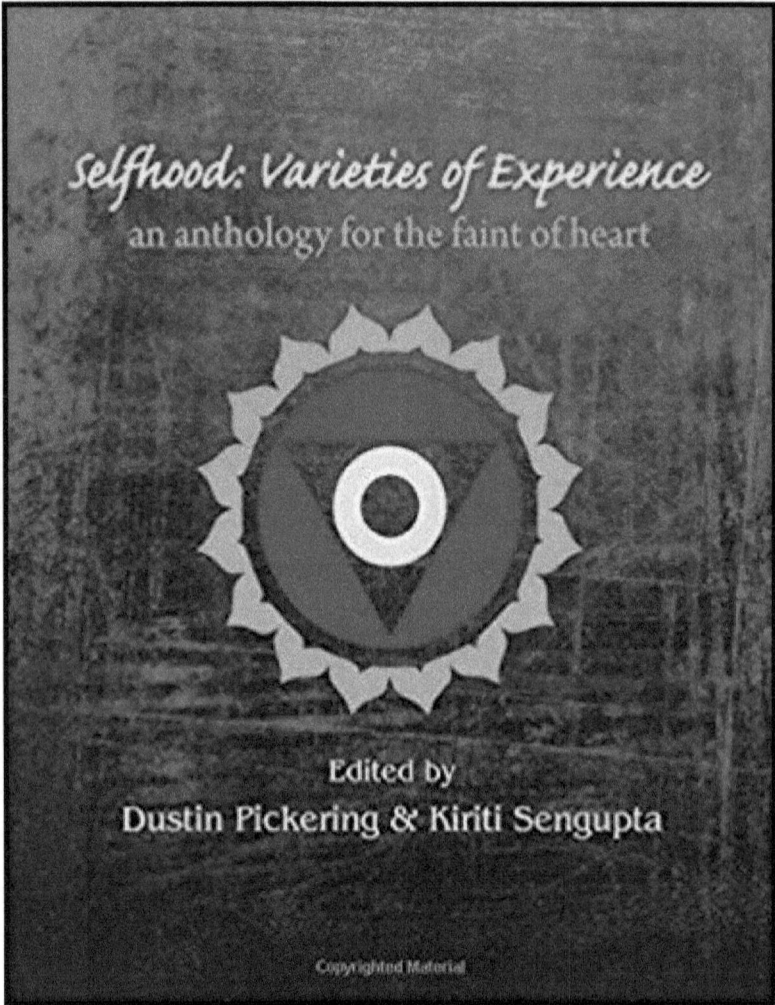

*Selfhood: Varieties of Experience* is a philosophical collection designed to compare outlooks of the Self as seen across the world. This stunning collection stayed an Amazon bestseller in new releases in poetry anthologies for two straight weeks.

Editors Kiriti Sengupta and Dustin Pickering worked together to draw verses from the Americas to India where concepts can be both different but compellingly alike. Introduction by Lyn Coffin.

# Also by TRANSCENDENT ZERO PRESS

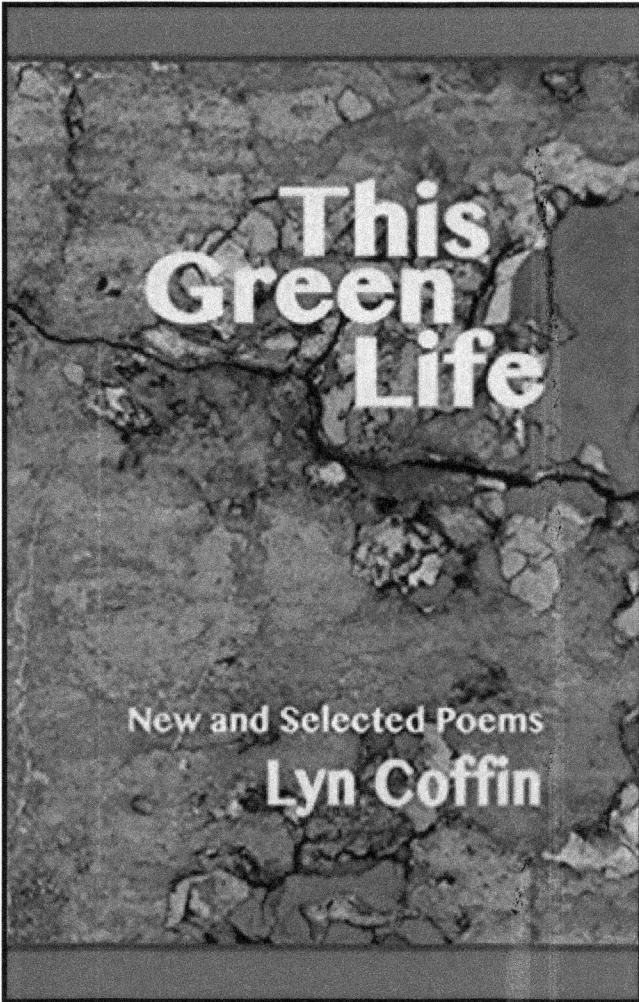

*This Green Life* is a tour de force from Lyn Coffin's previous collections. This stunning collection also includes new work never before published. This volume includes poetry from *Human Trappings, The Poetry of Wickedness, Crystals of the Unforeseen, East and West, Joseph Brodsky Was Joseph Brodsky, A Marriage Without Consummation,* and new poetry. It also includes the never before published "Rodin's Girl Friend."

# Also by TRANSCENDENT ZERO PRESS

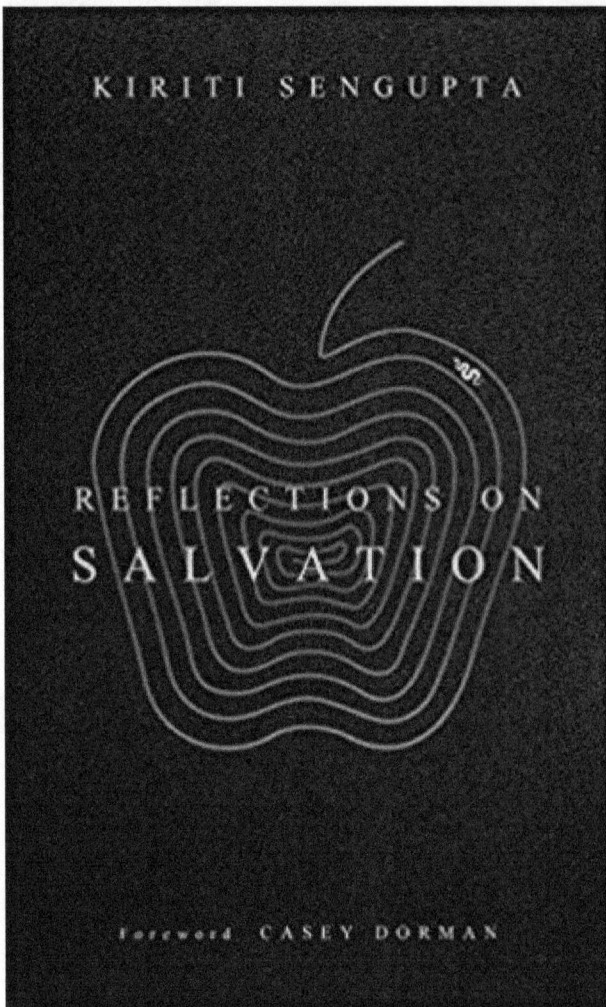

KIRITI SENGUPTA

REFLECTIONS ON
SALVATION

Foreword CASEY DORMAN

"In this new genre of 'Flash Wisdom' this book takes us gently and boldly into everyday life to scrutinize the beliefs we work out of, often with a touch of ironic humor that leads us to laugh at our foibles and brings us into a deeper understanding of what salvation might mean today." — Dr. Mary Madec [Ireland]